SECOND
ETRUSCAN
CAMP

Quirinal Hill

Capitoline
Hill

FORUM

SACRED WAY

Palatine
Hill

FIRST
ETRUSCAN
CAMP

River Tiber

Avetine Hill

SERVIAN WALL

ROME

Brave Cloelia

JANE LOUISE CURRY ~ Illustrated by JEFF CROSBY

Retold from the account in
THE HISTORY OF EARLY ROME
by the Roman historian Titus Livius

THE J. PAUL GETTY MUSEUM
• LOS ANGELES

King Larth Porsena, the Etruscan, looked out over the tents of his ten thousand soldiers and at his hundreds of horses and mules. "I am bored with this war," he growled. "I'll be glad to go home."

"I, too, my sweet," said his queen, and she patted his hand.

The king scowled across the River Tiber at the seven hills of the city of Rome. "Romans! They throw out our cousin Tarquin, their king, and then he nags me to win his city back for him. But even when I take Rome prisoner, what do these Romans say? 'Tell Tarquin to go twiddle his thumbs! We'll have no king at all!'"

"If I had Tarquin for king, I would say the same," said the queen as she poured her husband a cup of cold pear juice and cream.

King Larth gave a sigh. "I promised Tarquin. But the Romans would rather starve! Still, today we have agreed to agree. They will send us two hundred hostages and give up the Etruscan land they stole. We have promised to move back two miles toward our road home so that their farmers can come out to tend their fields and their flocks."

"Well done!" said his queen. "Even *one* mile closer to home is better than none."

The next day King Larth watched as the Roman hostages were led from the boats. "One hundred ninety-eight, one hundred ninety-nine, two hundred," the king counted. "By Fufluns!* The Romans have kept their word! Maybe they really do wish for peace." He thought for a moment. "Master Haruspex," he called out to his diviner of omens, whose job it was to read the future. "I consider that a good omen. Do you?"

"I do, King of Clevsin," said old Laris, the haruspex. "I see some here from the great clans of Rome. There are Fabii and Valerii . . . Pinarii . . . Cloelii . . ."

The Cloelii came last. First was Uncle Julius Cloelius, then his small son, Publius, his tall wife, Tullia, and his plump daughter, Julia. And, last of all, his niece, Cloelia.†

*Fufluns was the Etruscan god of wine.

†Pronounced klo-EE-lee-a.

The hostage camp had no wall or fence, but the Etruscan king's guards were everywhere. Young Cloelia felt like a mouse in a trap.

Her Uncle Cloelius was stiff and stuffy.

"Of *course* we'll be safe," he huffed. "King Larth now knows that Rome keeps its word, and we are his guarantee that it will keep the peace. Stand straight, Cloelia, and tuck in your chin!"

Aunt Tullia was snappish and sniffy. She glared all around. "That queen's face is painted! And the men strut like peacocks in their vulgar, showy robes. Oh! And the servant boys wear nothing at all! Disgusting! Look away, Cloelia!"

After supper, Cloelia slipped out through the dusk to climb into the top of the great fig tree beyond the last hostage tent.

Quiet as an owl on her perch, she looked out over the camp. She saw the great fields of tents, the horse pens, a straggle of rooftops down near the riverbank, and the ships. She watched lamps wink on in the windows of far-off Rome and torches flare in the camp close by.

And as she watched the guards on patrol, her eyes grew as round as an owl's, then as narrow as a clever cat's.

And she smiled.

After dark, Cloelia lay still in her bed for a long time and listened. When the tent grew quiet she threw off her cover and crept across to the nearest cot.

"Cousin?" she whispered. "Are you awake? I'm going home to Rome."

Julia's eyes blinked open wide. "Oh, Cloelia! You can't!"

"I can! If Uncle and Aunt had let me go home by myself, I wouldn't be here at all."

"But *now*? And *how*?"

"Not now. Tomorrow night." Cloelia's eyes gleamed in the dark. "There's a path down to the little town and the river, a path that the guards don't watch. Come swim home to Rome with me!"

Julia looked over toward her mother's bed. She hesitated for a moment. "I will," she said.

"I'll ask Virginia, too," said Cloelia.

"And Marcia!" whispered Julia.

"Yes! And Domitilla . . . and Lucia . . . and Livia!"

At noon the next day Aunt Tullia turned up her nose at the hostages' meal. "Etruscan food is too spicy," she announced. "Tonight we will cook our own!"

So she and her friends made a list and sent a woman to tell the guards what they needed. In no time at all (and to everyone's surprise), wine and oil, fresh coriander, young pigs and dried figs, vinegar and eggs, honey, pepper, and pears came by the cartload, all at King Larth's order. And two carts came with all of the things that the listmakers had forgotten: the kettles and knives, the firewood, and big, bronze braziers to cook on.

Aunt Tullia and Uncle Julius and their friends gave directions while the not-quite-as-important women chopped and measured and mixed, and the not-quite-as-important men butchered, built fires in the braziers, and baked bread in the coals.

The girls tidied the tents. The boys played at wrestling and harpastum.*
And Cloelia's whisper passed from girl to girl:

Tonight. In the moon shadow beneath the fig trees. Bare feet.
Nothing that jangles.

*Harpastum was a rough football game played with a very small ball.

At midnight Cloelia lifted the flap of the tent and slipped out. The camp was asleep. Sentry fires and torches glimmered here and there in the darkness, and a sliver of moon shone down on the camp.

Cloelia shrank back as a warning *scrunch-scrunch* of footsteps drew near and passed by. When the guard was gone, she slipped out and darted between the tents and away.

Julia came next.

And another girl-shadow . . .

and another . . .

Waiting in the darkness under the trees, Cloelia counted five, six . . . ten . . . twenty-three . . . thirty-two . . . forty!

Cloelia and her shadows tiptoed away from the trees single file and scurried to hide behind a row of cow sheds. The line flitted through the moonlight as swiftly as a slender snake but stopped still as a row of stones at the *clank* of a spear or the *slap* of a sandal.

"Who goes there?" roared a guard as a pebble rolled past him near the shed.

"Who goes there?" yelped another as a shadow flickered among the leaves in a vineyard.

"W-who g-goes t-there?" croaked a third as a scrap of cloud covered the moon and hid the heads that bobbed along behind a garden wall.

"Whoo-oo, whoo-oo," hooted an owl-voice from an olive tree.

Cloelia, then two . . . ten . . . twenty . . . forty girls crawled down a deep, dry ditch. They crept along behind a boatman's house near the River Tiber. Cloelia peered out to make sure the way was clear.

A stout sentry stalked up and down on the stone quay along the river's edge.

"Oh, no!" breathed Barbara. (Or Claudia. Or Flavia.)

Cloelia pointed to the two tall-prowed ships anchored near the riverbank. Then she pointed at the sky, where a great cloud was coming to cover the moon.

In the darkness, one by one, the girls slipped after Cloelia.

One by one they slithered down the bank, then slid like otters through the dark water between the ships.

And when the moon came out again, they were safe in the long ships' shadows.

"All together !" Cloelia whispered in the nearest ears. "Pass it on!"

"All together, pass it on," whispered away to the right.

"All together," went the whisper away to the left.

One . . . two . . . thirty-five . . . forty-one dark heads bobbed in the river. Eighty-two arms sliced through the water. Eighty-two feet fluttered fiercely.

"Who goes there?" shouted the stout sentry on the quay. "Ho, guards! Torches here! Guards! Torches!"

The girls paddled on. Plunged on. Raced on. Surged on.

"There!" shouted a guard.

"No, *there*!!" cried another. "Stop them!"

"SHOOT!" the captain shouted.

Arrows swished through the air. They stung the water. *Splash! Splish! Plash!*

In Rome the sentries on the city walls were the first to hear the shouts and see the torches swarm down to the river's edge.

They called to the captain of the guard, "The Etruscans are shooting at the river!"

The captain took a look and sent men to awaken the senators. "The Etruscans are shooting at girls out swimming!" the men told the half-asleep senators. Some senators came to look, and they sent messengers to call the consuls. The consuls came to look and saw that the strongest swimmers had already reached the shore. "To the river!" they cried. "Help those girls out of the water!"

The noise and the news brought out the citizens, too. They poured through the city gate to welcome the girls with glad cries of "Marcia!" or "Camilla!" or "Julia!"

And they wrapped them in dry clothes — and warm embraces.

In the Etruscan camp King Larth strode up and down in a rage. He waved his arms. He shouted at his general, Prince Arruns. The captain and corporal of the guard trembled at every word.

"Sentries who can't keep watch? Guards who can't guard? Archers who *cannot shoot*? I should have every man of them whipped! Tell me: were no guards posted at the hostage tents?"

"There were, Great King," Prince Arruns said in a very small voice. "But only at the tents of the men and boys."

"So our guards were eluded by a gaggle of girls? Outwitted by this crafty Cloelia? This child?"

"Indeed, it is so, Great King," mumbled the general and captain and corporal of guards.

"Arr-rr-gh!" roared the king. "Call my ambassador to me. I don't give a fig for the forty, but I will have this Cloelia. By great Herkle,* the girl is more of a danger than their Horatius!" †

*Herkle was the Etruscan name for Hercules.

†The Roman soldier Horatius single-handedly defended the bridge across the Tiber, holding back the Etruscans until the Romans could pull the bridge down.

King Larth's ambassador was rowed to Rome to present the king's angry demand: *Send the hostage Cloelia to me at once. If you don't, our treaty is broken and my army will sweep over Rome like a storm. If the girl comes, I shall return her to you. But she must come.*

"We have no choice," Cloelia's grandfather said gravely. "If the Etruscans return and can't break down our gates, they'll simply camp outside our walls again and wait for Rome to starve."

Cloelia's father nodded, but anger made his eyes bright. "Still, we won't send her back like a runaway slave; we'll *take* her back, and proudly!"

So they did, Cloelia's grandfather and father and all the great men of the family Cloelius. They crossed the Tiber in the only boat Rome could command.

As Cloelia stepped onto the quay and walked to meet King Larth's royal guard, the Cloelii watched with their heads held high.

See, their proud looks seemed to say. *Even the smallest of Romans is the equal of an Etruscan king!*

"So this is Cloelia!" King Larth Porsena growled. "A small person to be such a great nuisance."

"Thank you, King," said Cloelia.

King Larth's queen laughed and clapped her hands.

King Larth scowled. Then he laughed, too. "Ho! I like this Roman! She has courage enough for a troop of my flat-footed guards. Tonight, Cloelia, you will join us at our feast!"

There were toasted almonds and hazelnuts, chestnuts and pine nuts, bowls of fava beans and buttered peas. Plates of plump, stuffed mushrooms and flatbreads topped with spicy sausage and stringy cheese. Platters of baked mullet, squid, and eels, then roasted veal and lamb and suckling pig, and wild boar stuffed with figs.

When Cloelia couldn't take another bite, King Larth raised up his silver wine bowl. "Hear me, sons and daughters of great Clevsin, and drink to brave Cloelia!"

To Cloelia herself, the king said, "I have promised to send you home, but in honor of your cunning and courage, I now promise you something more. Tomorrow you may pick from the hostages another forty to take back with you to Rome. If the choosing is too hard—"

"No, King," Cloelia said loudly, for she guessed which hostages the king would most like to keep, for fear that one day they would wage war against him.

"I'll choose from among the boys."

The next morning the walls of Rome were lined with eager watchers. Would Larth Porsena keep his word? Or would he carry Cloelia away?

"Something's afoot!" they said, although there was nothing moving.

"Something's astir!" they cried, although there was nothing to see.

Then, "Listen! Horns!" came a cry from the Capitoline Hill.

"And drums!" came a shout from the fort on the Palatine Hill.

"Look! Banners!" came a call from the Servian Wall.

Down the Triumphal Way marched the trumpeters and drummers, carrying flags of crimson and gold. Down toward the boats by the river came the black horses and gold chariot of King Larth Porsena, with a dozen crimson-canopied carriages following him. Behind marched the soldiers of the great city of Clevsin, by the hundreds, the thousands, and still thousands more.

Rome fell silent in fear—until a small figure jumped down from beside the king, and forty others from the carriages behind.

"Cloelia! I see Cloelia!" cried Julia.

And a great shout rang out from the walls and hills of Rome. "Cloelia is bringing our Roman boys home!"

A great crowd met the boats at the wharf. At the front were the two consuls elected to govern Rome, the twelve lictors,* and all three hundred senators. Behind them were the Cloelii, then the relatives of the returning boys, and as many soldiers and citizens as could crowd through the gates.

The people cheered as the Etruscan ambassador led Cloelia ashore. They cheered as the boys poured off a second boat.

"What has happened?" the consuls shouted.

"All is well," the ambassador said, and he told of the king's gift to Cloelia. "The treaty is not broken. The war is over at last. And see," said he, "even now King Larth and his army are marching off toward the road to Veii."

The good news leaped from hill to hill. "Cloelia! Cloelia!" the crowds roared out. "We want Cloelia!"

Cloelia's father lifted her up onto his horse. The soldiers formed a guard of honor to parade her into the city. Behind came the boys, then the consuls, the lictors, and the three hundred senators. As the parade passed by, all of Rome gave a cheer and followed.

*Lictors were the consuls' bodyguards.

After a year or two, Larth Porsena sent the rest of the
hostages home from Clevsin. From that time forward,
he and Rome remained at peace.

The Senate paid to have a statue cast in bronze, the
first of its kind in Rome of a woman or a girl. The
bronze Cloelia sat astride a bronze horse at the top of the
Sacred Way, and the inscription on the statue's base read

CLOELIA FORTIS

which is Latin for CLOELIA THE BRAVE.

Text © 2004 Jane Louise Curry

Getty Publications
1200 Getty Center Drive
Suite 500
Los Angeles, California 90049-1682
www.getty.edu

Christopher Hudson, *Publisher*
Mark Greenberg, *Editor in Chief*

Project Staff
John Harris, *Editor*
Kurt Hauser, *Designer*
Elizabeth Zozom, *Production Coordinator*

Printed in Singapore by Tien Wah Press

Curry, Jane Louise.
   Brave Cloelia : retold from the account in The history of
early Rome by the Roman historian Titus Livius / Jane
Louise Curry ; illustrated by Jeff Crosby.
      p. cm.
   ISBN 0-89236-763-6 (Hardcover)
   1. Cloelia, 6th cent. B.C.–Juvenile literature. 2. Porsena,
Lars, 6th cent. B.C.–Juvenile literature. 3. Rome–History–
Republic, 510-265 B.C.–Juvenile literature. [1. Cloelia, 6th
cent. B.C. 2. Porsena, Lars, 6th cent. B.C. 3. Rome–History–
Republic, 510-265 B.C.] I. Crosby, Jeff, ill. II. Livy. Ab urbe
condita. III. Title.
   DG236.C58C87 2004
   937´.03´092--DC22

                                        2003026178

Etruria, the country of the Etruscans, lay between the River Tiber and the River Arno to the north of Rome. Across that land the ancestors of the Etruscans, a people known as the Villanovans, built their villages atop plateaus and isolated hills. By the time Rome was founded, in about 750 B.C., these Etruscan hilltop towns had grown into prosperous city-kingdoms.

Pisa

Florence

River Arno

Volterra

Cortona

Populonia

Chiusi
(Clevsin)

ELBA

Orvieto

River Tiber

Vulci

Tarquinia

Veii

Cerveteri

Rome

CORSICA

Tyrrhenian Sea

ITALY

Adriatic Sea

Naples

SARDINIA

Around 600 B.C. the Etruscan Lucius Tarquinius Priscus was elected king in Rome. He and his successors ruled there for almost a century, until the Romans expelled the cruel king Tarquin the Proud. In 506 B.C., the year of Cloelia's adventure, peace was finally established between Rome and the Etruscan king, Larth Porsena. But in the centuries that followed Rome steadily conquered the whole of Italy, town by town. In 27 B.C., after a thousand years, the Etruscan nation ceased to exist.

SICILY